JOHN JERNINGHAM'S

JOURNAL

JOHN JERNINGHAM'S JOURNAL

NEW YORK
CHARLES SCRIBNER & CO.
1871

More than a year ago Mrs. Jerningham put forth to the world the experiences of her early married life. Mr. Jerningham also kept a diary; and extracts therefrom are given in the following pages. As they refer to the relations between husband and wife, their mutual action and re-action upon each other, it is believed they will be of interest to the general public—especially to all who have entered into, or are about to enter into, the holy estate of matrimony.

JOHN JERNINGHAM'S JOURNAL.

PART I.

A PLIANT form, a pretty face,
  An airy, fairy, laughing thing,
That moved about with careless grace,
  Like little bird on active wing—
A sort of human butterfly,
Now going far, now hovering nigh ;
Yet still, while flitting here and there
  And smiling, nodding, talking fast,
So sweet her smile, so gay her air,
  You turned to watch her as she passed ;
And watching, found her pleasant look
The fairest page in Nature's book.

John Jerningham, don't be a fool!—
  More weighty matters claim your thought,
  Attend to business, as you ought!
Confound the thing! Neglect your rule—
  To give to work your working hours,
  To concentrate your ablest powers
On money, prices, shares, and stocks,—
Because a girl with golden locks
And scarcely yet escaped from school,
  Possessed a smiling, pretty face
  And moved about with airy grace!

A strong man swimming up the stream
  Must strike out bold, and never flinch!
No day is this to muse and dream;—
  The stoutest dare not give an inch!
For times are hard, and money's tight,
  And banks as sure as is our own
Will have a rather stiffish fight—
  And which shall stand, or fall, alone?

And we have been most madly sold
  By agents of our house, in Spain,
Who, for waste paper, drew our gold,
  Unmindful too, of coming strain;

A set of fools, with no more nous
  Than he who trumps his partner's ace!—
  And yet, forsooth, they have the face
To think them useful to the house!

'Tis sad, indeed, if house depends
Upon short-sighted, stupid friends;
For stupid friends hit doubly hard—
They take a fellow off his guard!

In truth, I have enough to do
  And where to turn I scarce can tell;—
Nought but a struggle pulls us through!—
  They said her name is Rosa Bell.

No matter, though, whate'er her name,
Or where she goes, or whence she came!

How many a house, that had been thought
  As certain as the Three Per Cents,
Has by the sudden blast been caught!
  And sore surprise, and sad laments,
And dire distress attend its fall.
  Such ruin lays full many low,
  Who can't recover from the blow;
Who rashly, madly, ventured all!

On business-men 'tis hard enough,
  But they can bear it, so to speak,
They take the smooth and take the rough;
  But oh! the old, the young, the weak,
My heart is wrung for these!—for these,
Who drain the sorrow to its lees!

'Tis not to them a business strife,
But serious throw for death or life,
And every 'panic' has its share
Of 'dead and wounded,' here or there!

The 'money-market,' 'stocks,' and 'shares,'
  And 'steady,' 'falling,' 'strong' or 'weak,'—
Ah! who can tell the hopes, the cares
  These simple words to thousands speak!
And so it must be still while gold
To measure wealth its place shall hold.

Why, John, what is the matter, man?—
Give way like this I never can!—
In every place, go where I will
That smiling face pursues me still!

Though many pretty girls I know
There ne'er was one that served me so!

How can it be?—'Tis too absurd!—
I will not bear it on my word!

Come, let us take the thing in hand—
  Let's look the matter in the face,
High time it is to understand
  The bearings of so strange a case!

I meet a little smiling girl,
  In years, indeed, she's but a child,
And might have found a priceless pearl!—
  Such nonsense drives one almost wild!
For truly, I have not much doubt
  This pretty girl's a silly chit;
I should not fail to find it out
  If I could study her a bit.—
When work is slack, and I am free
I'll go again—I'll go and see.

When this rough time is tided o'er
I'll run away from town once more.—

I half engaged, indeed, to spend
My holiday with that old friend,
Where first the pretty girl I met,
Whose pleasant laughter haunts me yet.

The fear is gone, the pressure past,
  And I can freely breathe again!
A strain like this, it could not last
  Or man could never bear the strain!

Well! we, and others, held our own.
  By Jove! how near were we let in!
And if the danger had been known
  The danger had still greater been.

If we had failed then others fell,
  I thought of that and did my best,
And what I did—it answered well!
  'Tis over now! and I can rest.

A private letter. Oh, I see—
  Yes, I might take my holiday,
There is not much to hinder me ;
  And Johnson writes a line to say,
He and his wife expect me down
When I can get away from town.

Ah, I remember!—I had meant
  On their kind help to throw myself
When I was, for a time, intent
  On studying that little elf
Who in my brains would flit about,
Till weightier matters drove her out.

For my hard work has gained the day;
  And still hard work must be my lot.—
But surely I might get away,
  So I will go—why should I not?

I'll take the Johnsons at their word,
  Have country air and exercise ;—
Then I shall see, too, how absurd
  It was to let the laughing eyes
And flitting form of that young girl
Put all my senses in a whirl!

Ah! this is good! I draw it in,
  A full, long, breath of pure, fresh air!
To stay in town would be a sin!
  Why is not country everywhere?

This pure, fresh air it is so fine,
  It brightens cheek, and lip, and eye,
A draught of dear old Nature's wine,
  And we can never drain it dry!

A long-drawn breath expands the chest
  And makes the freshened pulses beat,
It lulls excited nerves to rest,
  And puts a man upon his feet!

Happy the swains with rustic health,
  Who care not how the 'stocks' may go,
Rich in their very scorn of wealth!—
  But yet, perchance, a little slow!

Oh! if I only had the pow'r
  On breezy down, in shady wood,
To spend my every waking hour!—
  I really don't believe I should!

For though I'm glad to get away,
  With nothing in the world to do.
And find the first a pleasant day,
  I weary in a day or two.

I hope they'll send my letters down,
When free from business what is life !—
I got the latest news in Town,
And brought some fish for Johnson's wife.

I rise betimes, and go downstairs
So light of step, so void of cares,
And hungry too !
A freshness in the country air
Makes farmers relish plainer fare
Than townsfolk do !

Where are the papers? What's the news?
They 'don't see much except Reviews,'
And 'read *them* through' ! !
They only have one post a day !—
The office too so far away—
How can they do !

I don't deny your rightful wealth
Is that which keeps a man in health,
  Food—corn—and that;
But people surely ought to know
How shares and money-market go,
  'Buoyant' or 'flat'!—

Yet, after all, why, what are stocks
When you compare them with the flocks
  That graze around?
We cannot live except we eat,
We get our bread, we get our meat
  From off the ground.

There's good and ill in every case—
  This bracing air at least is charming!—
Johnson is wedded to the place
  And prides himself upon his farming.

We took a ramble, looked at stores
  Of hay and corn—a pleasant sight,
We passed the morning out of doors
  And came in with an appetite.

How tranquil Johnson's daily course!—
  Of crops how learnedly he talks!
(I wonder where he bought that horse?)
  We have good rides, or famous walks—
Of country air he gets his fill,
And what a breather up that hill!

To him no anxious times, no care,
Nothing to take him unaware,
Nothing to vex him or to worry,
No eager dread, no fear, no flurry!

A country life's the life to live,
And country air the air to give
  Muscle and bone!

Our fathers may have thought of this!—
The country would not be amiss
   Ere Town was known!

If our whole island were a town,
Old England's glory would come down,
   For pluck and strength
Want early hours, and wholesome air,
And simple, good, substantial fare,
   Or fail at length!

I find it getting rather slow,—
  I thought it would be when I came!
Town has so much that's fresh to show.
  But here—'tis day by day the same!

Well, it is wonderful and strange
  In country life, what people see!
I cannot do without a change,
  The City is the place for me.

Now, as you walk along a street
There's always something new to meet;
But here it is so blank and tame,
The wood, the river—just the same!

The same high hills, the same low meads !
  A shift of wind becomes a boon.—
Yet Johnson likes the life he leads !
  'Twould settle me—and pretty soon !

But here to find some change one tries—
  'Tis hot or cold, or dry or wet ;
And in the morn the sun must rise,
  And in the evening he must set ;

And if he sets in glorious hues
  Fair weather we may hope to see,
And this, alas ! is all the news—
  If news it is—that reaches me !

One never knows the time of day,
  Or where to go, or what to do,
The hours pass wearily away—
  Which early train will take me 'through' ?

Ah, I have seen sweet Rosa Bell!
  And now I know
  What charmed me so,
What forms her witchery,—her spell!
'Tis not the dazzling pink and white,
  Nor sparkling eyes, nor golden hair;—
And though a merry, dancing sprite,
  Kittens would meet and beat her there!
But she is very fair to view—
Like Mother Eve when worlds were new—
Fair by the light of inner grace
Reflected in her changeful face;
The heaven within her upraised eye,
  The sudden look of sweet surprise
To master that which passes by,
  And all the love that dormant lies;
For she is but an opening flower!—
  She's on the threshold of her life!—

And she will be a noble dower
   To him who takes the girl to wife.

All that is sweet, and good, and fair,
Are folded in and nestled there,
And ask but time, and warmth, and space,
To open out in fullest grace
Of 'perfect woman, nobly planned
To warn, to comfort, and command!'

She met us, and she stopped to talk;
   And, strange enough! remembered me;—
And hoped I'd had a pleasant walk,
   And said she was quite glad to see
I had escaped again from Town.—
But this, of course, I must put down
To mere politeness, for we say
As much as this is every day.—
She looked as if she meant it, though,
And gave a beaming smile, I know.

I'm glad I've seen her once again,
  For now I understand the charm
That kept her image in my brain,
  And filled me with a strange alarm.—
'Tis that her beauty, barely ripe,
Made her stand forward as the type
Of what is sweet, and fair, and good
In early opening womanhood.

She makes me think of Joan of Arc
  And fair Godiva, both in one !—
Grace Darling, in her fragile bark,
  Did but what this fair girl had done
Had she belonged to such a grade—
And been, too, somewhat stouter made !

Are there not strange affinities
  That permeate all time and space ?
Some, in the old divinities
  Embodiment of them can trace.—

'Tis said that Nature makes a pair,
And two-fold life is everywhere.—
Where dwells the one who could to me
A sort of second-being be?

A dinner-party! What a bore!
  Now Johnson might have spared me that!
And I have told him o'er and o'er
  I much prefer a quiet chat!

I can't escape, at any rate;—
  I should have got away, indeed
But did not know until too late!—
  Nor can I an engagement plead!

I scarcely yet had ceased to fume,
  But smoothed my brow, and calmed my air,
And having reached the drawing-room,
  Found—Rosa, and her father, there.

And me to him they introduce,
  I hear they call him Major Bell,—
A tall, old man, both neat and spruce—
  A sort of antiquated swell.

He had not much, indeed, to say,
  Answered with yeses, and with noes,
And so I quickly got away
  And went and stood by little Rose.

And little Rose looks up and smiles,
  And seems to brighten when I come !—
Is she a witch with artful wiles ?—
  What can have made me almost dumb ?

And yet it would be well to speak,
  To utter something smart and gay,
And bring the dimple to her cheek—
  But all my words had fled away !

The dinner—like too many such,
  You had not room to move your arms,
Your neighbour you must almost touch—
  For me these crowds possess no charms.

Some that give dinners seem to think,
  More than the tables fairly seat
Will fill up pleasure to the brink !—
  Their own good wishes they defeat.

Crowds at a race are very well,
  But not at dinner, or at ball.—
A married man took Rosa Bell,
  And I—took no one in at all.

They played at croquet on the lawn—
  I stopped awhile to watch the game,
  I thought it very poor and tame,
And turned to leave them, with a yawn !—
But Rosa Bell then stood by me,
  And chattered gaily as she stood ;
Before she went I got to see
  A game at croquet might be good !
She asked me if I did not play,
  And volunteered the rules to teach ;
But I replied, I could not stay,
  Which surely was a stupid speech ;—
Especially as I remained
  Upon the ground at least an hour !—
I felt my footsteps were restrained
  By some unknown, resistless power !

I watched her play—she played it well,
  And knocked the painted balls about,
Her eyes were bright
With true delight
When to her some advantage fell;
  She gave a merry little shout
  At putting others to the rout!—
When she was 'home' and once more free
She came again and talked to me.

I liked the laughter in her eyes,
I liked the glow of exercise
Upon her cheek; and, as she play'd
Her feet a pretty picture made,
They are such dainty, tripping feet!—
  But language there has made a slip,
  For feet like hers would never *trip*,
They're far too clever, and too neat!

Her beauty comes out very well
  When you can catch it in repose
At church we fronted Major Bell,—
  And next to him, his daughter, Rose.

As on her cheek the lashes rest,
I think I like that style the best ;
But when I see her earnest eyes
In them a heaven of beauty lies !
So pure are they 'that from their ray
Dark Vice would turn abashed away.'

I almost thought to-day to trace
A sort of young-Madonna face !
All undeveloped, giving scope
For much of fancy, as of hope,
Dependent for its fashioning
On what the coming years may bring.

An Archery-meeting ; would I go ?
  I would.—It is a fine old sport—
You think of Robin Hood, you know,
  And William Tell—and all, in short,
Who drew, without a miss or flaw,
A longer bow than now we draw.

Toxopholites degenerate
  To me they seemed, that merry band ;
They mostly were effeminate,
  And did not strive to understand.

I could not praise their skill at all,
  Scarce one among them aimed to touch ;
The shafts at random seemed to fall—
  The bull's-eye did not suffer much !

The girls, though, made a pleasant chatter,
  And wore a pretty dress of green ;
They thought their failure did not matter—
  And that fair creature was their queen.

The arrows wildly went astray,
  And some fell wide, and some fell short ;—
It is not mastered in a day,
  This fine, old, noble English sport!

They could not hit the centre blot
  With careless aim and idle hands ;—
And Johnson says the safest spot
  Is always—where the target stands.

The shooting was absurdly bad—
  I rather liked their fancy dress—
And they were all as gay and glad
  As if it were a great success !

So, on the whole, I don't repine
  At having gone—it was as well—
'Twas all that offered—and—in fine,
  I saw again fair Rosa Bell.

And when that pretty maid I see
  In drawing-room, or field, or wood,
She talks most pleasantly to me—
  For which I think her very good.

She talks to me—yes, that's the fact—
  My speech her presence drives away—
With strange stupidity attacked
  I cannot find a word to say!

But she likes well enough to chat.—
  Why, John, what can you be about,
To let a little girl like that
  Put all your senses to the rout!

The pleasant days will hurry on ;
  Why can't we make the moments stay?
And I, alas ! must soon be gone—
  How quickly comes that wretched day !

It is not good to dwell alone—
  So God, who did our nature plan,
To whom our every want is known,
  Said of the first, the new-made man.

The lions pair, the eagles mate,
  The birds build nests in hedge and tree.—
'Tis vain to fight against one's fate !—
  I wonder if she'd marry me ?

I do not know which way to ask,
  I have no notion how to woo ;
It cannot be a pleasant task—
  But others manage to get through.

Oh, she is very beautiful !
  Would I could call her all my own !
A loving wife, and dutiful !—
  I cannot bear to live alone !

I'm fairly caught !—I cannot tell
  How much I love this pretty Rose !
My hopes I quell, and ring their knell,
  Unless I venture to propose !

'Love when 'tis true needs not the aid
  Of sigh nor oaths to make it known ;
And, to convince the cruel'st maid
  Lovers should use their love alone.

So Sedley says.—If this is all
  Love, of himself, must make it plain.—
How will the time of parting fall?—
  And shall I ever come again?

Oh, for some happy hour and chance
  To tell her all that's in my mind,
Some lonely walk, some rustic dance!—
  I think she would not prove unkind!

The thing is over, it is done!
I've staked the stake—but have I won?—
I have not spoken as I meant,
In sooth, I am but half content;
I could not all my passion tell,
For I proposed to—Major Bell!
It happened we were left alone,
  I thought the Major sounded me;
I therefore made my wishes known,
  And now await my destiny!—
Her father took my offer well;
Of course, 'twas not for him to tell
How she might feel; but in his air
Was something to forbid despair.—
He must have meant me to propose,—
But what about dear little Rose?

He was too smooth and too polite—
  I like a fellow out-of-hand!
I fear I have not acted right,
  To speak to one so smooth and bland.—
But it is over!—Nor to-day
Can I see Rose, for she's away;
To-morrow morning I must go,
The Major says, my fate to know.

Oh! Time, how senseless is the one
  Who represents you taking flight!
For me you neither fly nor run,
  You lamely limp along to-night!—
How can I sleep, how can I rest
With all this anxious doubt oppressed?—
For if she should not smile on me—
  She always smiles, meet when we may—
Let this a happy omen be!—
  My ecstasy I cannot say,
If she, my tender little dove,
Accepts, and can return my love!

She is so fair, so sweet, so good,
  And I—as happy as a boy !
I have been running in the wood,
  I climbed a tree for very joy !

I shouted till the woods replied,
  I shouted then at their reply ;
I could have halloo'd till I died,
  For who so gay, so glad as I !—

I've said at last what was to say,
  And now I hold the darling's word !
Oh ! quickly dawn thou brightest day
  That brings me home my little bird !—

I found her looking very sweet,
And half in blushes, half in tears,
As if afraid my love to meet—
And so I strove to calm her fears;

And told what she already knew,
And waited till she answered me;—
But when they came her words were few,
And checked by maiden modesty.

I liked her better in this guise
Than had she smiled as first she did;
I sought to see her angel eyes,
But they were veiled by downcast lid.

A sweeter Rose is this than she
Of whom we read—the Gardener's daughter,
Whom Juliet sent the man to see—
And he no sooner saw than sought her.

Johnson declares he's very glad,
 And Johnson's wife looked pleased and sly ;—
They'd surely set me down for mad
 If they but knew how pleased am I!

I feel my happy heart expand,
 My sympathies go out to all!—
There's not a being in the land
 But I could now a brother call!

For she is mine! Dear, blushing Rose,
 That scarcely could her answer give!—
And mine the earnest hope, God knows,
 To guard this treasure while I live!

I'm back at work—again in Town,
  How different my coming life!
I little thought, when I went down,
  To look about and get a wife.

Of changes time is very full—
  How seldom can we much foresee—
Whilst by his horns I took the bull,
  Upon his horns the bull took me!

Are there not hidden mysteries
  Our foresight mocking, and our sense?
How frequent are the histories
  Where seeming chance is Providence!

Oh! it is very sweet to own
I live not in myself alone!—

Her happy life is wrapped in mine,
  And pulse for pulse and breath for breath,
So close shall love our lives entwine
  We two are only one till death!—
And after death 'tis ours to be
Together in Eternity.

Her face no longer haunts me here,
With mocking smiles for ever near,
Or peeps from unexpected nooks
When I am busy with my books.
Down in my heart of hearts she lives,
And cheery warmth and strength she gives!
For all my being is astir
With thoughts and hopes that spring from her!

The rapture of the parting kiss!—
  I held her to my throbbing heart,
And took that sweet foretaste of bliss!—
  It made it worth the while to part.

But lovers who must part for years,
  Who go across the dreary seas,
What anguish in their falling tears !—
  Ah ! from my soul I pity these.

They part, and dare not hope to meet,
  Or hope, and find their hope is vain ;—
No joy for them, the woe to cheat,
  No pleasure to outweigh the pain !

I had, before I came away,
  An interview with Major Bell ;
He seemed to have a hand to play—
  I do not like him over well.

In open field you have the right
  To make good running when you can ;
The Major's grasp is very tight—
  Poor chances for a weakly man !—

Unlike her father, darling Rose!
  Her generous nature is her own;
Her every look and word disclose
  No guile, no art, to her is known!—

Like parent stem becomes the flower,
  Sparrow like sparrow seems to be,
But man receives a richer dower
  In infinite variety.

How seldom find we form and face
  Another face and form repeat!—
I love the difference to trace
  When passing through the crowded street;

And every differing face and form
  Its differing life and nature bears;—
Knew we the laws, no sudden storm
  In man would take us unawares.

Oh! quickly dawn thou happy day
When I shall call this angel, wife!
With her my own, come then what may,
There must be sunshine in my life!

I have a cosy little nest
Fit for my bird, my sweetest Rose;—
I think the people did their best
Its pretty fittings to dispose.

I knew not half so much before
Of carpets, curtains, poles, and rings;—
I used to deem it once a bore
To hear about such trivial things.

But now—for Rose—no pains too great,
No cares too small, that give her pleasure!—
I like to stand and contemplate
This casket for my valued treasure.

Oh! happy day, come soon, come soon,
  When darling Rosa will be mine!—
I'm longing for the honeymoon!
  I mean to take her up the Rhine.

'All thoughts, all passions, all delights,
  Whatever stirs this mortal frame,
All are but ministers of Love
  And feed his sacred flame.'

And high, indeed, his flame will mount,
  And scatter brightness on the way,
When I have nothing more to count
  To reach my wedding-day!

I weary of that wretched train!
  So many journeys to and fro!
Always to go and come again!—
  The very porters seem to know!

And now, whenever I run down,
  So fully is she occupied
With mantle, bonnet, skirt or gown,
  That I am almost thrust aside!

But should not holy marriage be
  A greater thought than handsome dress!—
These trifles hold her back from me—
  They seem to make her love me less.

I envy flounce and furbelow,
  And trimming, veils, and gloves, and lace;—
They occupy her more, I trow,
  Than can be good in such a case.

When Adam woke and saw his Eve,
  And loved his helpmeet, pure and fair,
No fuss like this arose to grieve
  And come between the happy pair!

But now the wedding—which we know
  As life-long tie of heart to heart
Has dress, and gaiety, and show
  To constitute its chiefest part!

No matter; it will bring about
  A time that can for all atone;
For when the wedding-bells ring out,
  I speed away—and not alone!

I took her down a pretty set
  Of pearls, for my pure pearl to wear—
I think I see her smiling yet!—
  I hope they'll suit a girl so fair.

On them she looked with loving eyes,
  Delighted was she with my choice,
And me she kissed in glad surprise!—
  It made my inmost heart rejoice!

The day at last is drawing near,
 The day for which I long have sighed ;
I pant with joy, I pant with fear—
 I go to claim my lovely bride !

PART II.

BOUND by the tie of man and wife–
  Whatever troubles may befall—
'Tis ours to know that fullest life
  Where each to each is all in all.—
My darling Rose, my gentle dove,
  I cannot tell my happiness
In knowing I have gained thy love ;
  Nor all my gratitude express
To think that I am one with thee—
  That through the change of coming years
We two are one—and cannot be
  Alone again in hopes or fears !
And may we, as we forward go
  Together, and together still,
The holiest, purest pleasure know,
  The brightest phase of life fulfil !

Again I see my blushing bride
Before the altar, at my side ;
Her gentle air, her timid look,
When I her slender finger took
And placed the ring ! I gave my troth
  To love and cherish her till death,
And she pledged hers ; and there to both
The priest our several duties read.—
  I did not freely draw my breath
Till it was done, and we were wed !

For I had felt it far too dear,
  Too sweet a draught for me to sip,
Thought some ill fate would interfere
  And snatch the cup when at my lip ;—
Nor could I drive away this dread
Till she was mine, and fairly wed !

The wedding guests, the bridesmaids there,
That seemed our happiness to share,

They fluttered round her, and she stood
  A Queen amid the graceful throng,
A thousand times more choice and good
  Than any maiden sung in song!
A pretty scene!—A happy day,
  Which still to happier days led on!—
But I was glad to get away
  And with my darling wife be gone.

My wife's remarks are very droll,—
  And then, the questions that she asks !
Are they from ignorance ?—or soul,
  And genius ?—*That* has many masks !

It strikes me she is little taught—
  No matter, she is very sweet ;
'Twas not a learned wife I sought,
  Love will all other teachers beat.

I could not have a happier task
  Than her light studies to direct,—
To every question she can ask
  A ready answer she'll expect !

Her mind is like an opening flower,
  And I shall be the Zephyr bland,

To breathe thereon with quickening power,
  And make the tender leaves expand.

And she will catch the hue, the tone,
  That ever nearest she shall find,
And thus become still more my own,
  For we shall be but one in mind!

A growing fear possesses me,
An anxious thought distresses me!—
'Tis but a look, a tone, an air,
And yet I wonder what is there!—
Is it a cloud that's creeping up?
A dash of bitter in the cup?
The 'little rift within the lute'?
The 'pitted speck in garnered fruit'?
Yet if I ask me what? or why?
No ready words give quick reply.—

'Tis vague alarm, 'tis coward fear ;
It will not open summons hear,
But hiding, slyly throws a dart
With careful aim at tender part.

A kind of want, a sort of care
Will hang about her unaware—
As though her inner being pined
For some great good it fails to find !—
A little matter, very slight,
  I cannot grasp it, though I see.—
It floats about, it hides the light,
  It makes some moments dull to me !

Would I possessed a potent charm !—
But is she ill ?—a new alarm !—
I questioned her, she hung her head ;
She only wanted change, she said.
If this the wrong, we must away !—
Back came her smiles, and she was gay.

She wanted change! With change oppressed,
I should have thought she wanted rest!
And so I hastily took fright
At what a journey will put right!

My little wife is singing gaily;
She loves to sing, and laugh, and chatter;
We move about, we're moving daily,
And there is nothing now the matter.

And she is charmed with all she sees,
And everything to her is new,
The merest trifles serve to please,
The child exclaims at every view!

And many a question puts to me,
  And mine is all her strange delight!—
It is a something grand to see
  A little wife so glad and bright!

And still how readily she'll look
  For information and for news,
As if I were a clever book
  Which she delighted to peruse!

And her intelligence is great!—
  The richest ground, though lying fallow!—
I wonder by what freak of fate
  Her learning chanced to be so shallow?

But though she's quick, and sweet and fair
  The charm of charms—all else above—
It fills my heart, it revels there—
  That I possess her fullest love!

That all her being turns to mine ;
  That growing liker, side by side,
We shall together, cloud or shine,
  ' From happy years to happier glide.'

Now comes another little fear
To enter in and nestle here,
But I, without the least delay,
Drive this ill-favoured sprite away.—
I would not have the slightest slur,
The slightest censure, passed on her !

I do not want her like a prude !—
Why will this whispering fear intrude ?
I might be rather glad to see
Her manner just a shade less free.—

Not that she means to be too bold,
No, Rosa free from blame I hold!
It is the present style and tone,—
I do not think it good, I own.

My mother, now—those times are past,
Manners and fashions will not last,
Girls have become a little fast!
To copy mothers would be slow!
Still there are things should never go;
And womanly reserve—the nice
And ready instinct, thwarting vice—
Is one of them. I love to see
The outworks held by modesty;
The quick alarm that seems to tell
You cannot storm the citadel!

I do not blame my dearest Rose,
It is the way the fashion goes,
And against fashion how convince?
But I confess it makes me wince

To see my wife so freely chat
With strangers at hotels, and that.—
That Frenchman, first, on board the boat—
But he is only one to quote—
It was presuming when the man
At once to talk to Rose began !
She should have known the proper way
To keep such insolence at bay !
She might have checked him with a look,
  And quietly have been polite ;
She laughed at his mistakes, and took
  The greatest pains to put him right !
And seemed about as pleased as he,
And was, I thought, almost too free !

I do not wish my wife to fetter,
But more reserve would please me better
If she were less accessible,
Her spirits more repressible,
A something there, a sort of grace,
To make all people know their place !

She's so attractive, and so fair,
Men turn to watch her everywhere,—
And she is pleased because they stare!
Were I a woman, now, I think
From such attention I should shrink.

She means no harm, but, to my taste,
This confidence is much misplaced.
The code she goes by seems to be—
With men be at your ease, and free;
Love where you love, and treat the others
As if they were your friends and brothers!

At home! —A very charming word
  Has home become to me,
So sweet, its like was never heard
  In days of liberty.

There's one to watch my coming home,
  To meet me with a smile;
In truth, I have no need to roam
  My leisure to beguile.

But breakfast over, I'm away,
  And only back to dine.—
I wonder how she spends the day,
  To what her tastes incline?

I almost envy her, indeed,—
 So much as she might do!—
There are so many things to read,
 I scarce can look them through.

But I my duty must not shirk
 Nor do my duty ill,
For now I've double cause to work,
 And work with double will.

To have a second life that lives
 For you, and you alone,
Repeats your pleasures, and it gives
 A greater of its own!—

I do believe Rose scarcely reads
 A Paper or Review;
She'd rather work a mat with beads
 Than look a column through;

She'd rather play a silly dance
   That has so little in it,
Than give to matters of finance,
   Or politics, a minute!—

Well, never mind, she's very sweet
   And very dear to me!
I love to watch her, bright, and neat,
   At dinner and at tea.

And when she pours me out my tea,
   The tea it is so good!—
It never was like this to me
   In days of bach'lorhood!

I often take another cup,
   To have her pour it out,
And sip, and drink it slowly up,
   And keep the things about.—

And when I have to say good bye,
  I tear myself away.—
My business over, back I fly,
  Without the least delay!

My wife's first ball to-morrow night,
And she is wild with gay delight,
And occupied about her dress,
Which she would have a grand success!—
I hope my friends will take to her—
  But that they cannot fail to do—
That she's most winning, I aver,
  And then she is so pretty too!

I must not have her dance too much,
  I cannot let her waltz at all.
I ventured on my views to touch
  When we were talking of the ball.—
Though some may say I'm too precise,
  I have the right to draw a line;—
I do not think round dances nice—
  At least for Rosa, now she's mine.

The ball is over! Would to Heaven
  I had not taken Rosa there!
This horrid pain so roughly given,
  And not one jot she seems to care!

Before she went her evening dress
  Annoyed me—cut by far too low,
I strove to make the evil less,—
  Without a scarf she should not go!

And she was almost in a passion,
  She did not like to put it on,—
But this is not a point of fashion,—
  She took it off when I was gone!

Now Lady Græme is most refined,
  Such dressing would her taste offend,
And I had always set my mind
  On having her for Rosa's friend.

I felt inclined to stop away—
  And now I truly wish we had!
But Rosa counted on the day,—
  I did not like to make her sad.

Beside, I never should have guessed
  She can't be trusted out of sight!—
I am astonished and distressed
  At learning what I learned to-night!

I played a rubber, and returned
  To find her—whirling in a waltz!
And all my wishes coldly spurned,
  And all her promises made false!

How dared she! With her smiling face
  Close to the man's! her shoulders bare!—
He clasped her in the giddy race,
  His whiskers almost touched her hair!

I could have dashed amid the crowd
  To tear her from his circling arm!
I checked myself—I felt too proud
  To make a scene—to cause alarm.

I brought her home without delay,
  My rage I hardly could conceal,
I think she pleaded still to stay,—
  Nor seemed the least remorse to feel.

My thoughts on deep upbraidings ran,—
  But I suppressed them when I spoke;
She answered lightly—as she can—
  She seemed to think it all a joke.

That I had told her not to waltz
  She half denied—or did not care—
But this pretence was weak and false,—
  She coolly set about her hair.—

I never felt more deeply hurt!—
  My wishes trampled in the dust!—
In power of vain and giddy flirt
  It is not wise one's peace to trust!

I've taken measures to prevent
  Recurrence of this dreadful pain—
She shall have leisure to repent
  Before she goes to balls again!

For then and there did I decline
  The invitations for each ball—
If she regards no wish of mine
  I will not take her out at all;

So, at her desk I sat me down
  And wrote replies, constrained and glum,
To Lady Vaux, and half the Town,
  Declaring that we could not come.

I rang the bell, the letters sent
  For posting in the nearest box.—
And then I told her what I meant—
  That notes despatched to Lady Vaux,

And Mrs. Payne, and Colonel Vane
  From those engagements set us free.—
Nor will I take her out again
  Till she has learned to study me!

At breakfast time she gave my cup
  With stiff politeness ; had she shown
The least desire to make it up
  I should have yielded, I must own.—
I waited till the hour was past,
And went unreconciled at last !

I strove to-night to break the ice
  By asking how the day was spent.
Her answers were not free, nor nice,—
  I wholly failed in my intent.—
She did not read, she did not play,
  For what she *did* I'm at a loss.—
She did not, surely, fret all day
  Because I scolded and was cross ?

My interference she resented—
That I had spoken I repented—
I could not bear her altered look,
And turned for refuge to a book.

I long to snatch her to my heart
  And kiss to smiles that ugly frown,
But while she plays this injured part
  She would but coolly put me down.—
And I am sorry now I wrote
  Those notes so hastily last night.—
  Her look of sorrow and affright
When she was told—my heart it smote,
And haunts me still !—'Tis past recall—
  Well, I must ask her pardon there ;
I'll take her to some other ball
  If the round dances she'll forswear.

Another day has passed away
  And still this distance and this gloom!
Where is the creature, bright, and gay,
  That gave a charm to every room?—
She meets me with a cool good-morrow,
  Politely formal at each meal,
Shows more of anger than of sorrow—
  She cannot guess at what I feel!
No loving tone, or look, or kiss,
How can I live a life like this!
And live it why?—Because she did
The only thing I had forbid,
And took to sulking when I chid!

'Tis very hard to be at strife
 With one we love ! Each word unkind
Cuts to the heart like cruel knife,
 And rankles after in the mind.

And where we blame, and still love on,
 And cannot all the blame forget,
Our anger shall not soon be gone,
 Two-edg'd it is, and doubly whet;

For we are angered first at wrong
 Borne by ourselves, then far above
This anger, other, lasting long,
 For fault abiding where we love.

Can she be made of flesh and blood
  And bear on terms like these to live?
The tranquil beast that chews the cud
  Could not a calmer picture give;
Except that I at times have thought
  She seems afraid to meet my eye,
And looks as if she had been caught
  In something wrong or something sly!

Oh! Rosa, let me still be sure
  That no deceit can ever dwell
Within that breast I thought so pure!
  For thee to doubt, would faith expel
And I should know not where to cast
An anchor in the whelming blast!

Another day shall not pass by
  Till I have spoken out my mind!
Rosa may sulk, or she may cry,
  Or call me cruel and unkind;
I will not have our wedded life
Embittered by this hateful strife,
I'll take to task my little wife!—
I'll show her what her duties are,
  And where she fails, and I am pained.
Her life and mine she shall not mar
  By false resentment, overstrained.—
The right she must be made to see,
And she will surely yield to me.

She does not love me! Oh, the pang,
 The thrilling anguish of that thought!-
Envenomed bite of deadly fang!—
 It is with madness fraught!

I spoke to her.—I would not let
 Our mutual life drag on in pain!
A word to her I hoped would set
 The matter right—make peace again.

I deemed it but a lingering haze
 That hung between, and hid the light—
This blown away, our future days
 Would, like our former ones, be bright.

I talked to her of love and truth,
  Of patience and forbearance too-
I said her ignorance—her youth,
  Should yield to one who better knew.

I tried to paint the happy life
  That could be led alone by those
Who, in the tie of man and wife,
  Considered duties that arose.—

She answered like a silly child,
  Trying to make a childish joke;
At this I felt provoked and wild—
  It was with purpose that I spoke.

But suddenly there came the thought
  She does not love me, for she knows
No sympathy with me!—I sought
  To prove me wrong, and questioned Rose.—

For if she loved me, soon or late
  Would all come right, no matter when ;
Thirsting at once to know my fate,
  I asked her if she loved me then.—

And did she love me ?—No reply !—
  Sharp answers stab ! hard words may kill !
But *silence* to *this* question !—Why,
  It is intensity of ill !

To be my wife she would not come
  Without some answering love for me ?—
The stilly silence struck me dumb,
  I could not fail its drift to see !

And did she dare the future stake,
  Unloving come to share my life,
And calmly, coldly undertake
  The holy duties of a wife !

Then as the truth shone boldly out
  On other wrong its light it threw,-
Her father brought the thing about!
  And was not I imprudent too?

For charmed by figure and by face
  I read therein the good I wanted,
Caught by her witchery and grace,
  Her love I almost took for granted.

But now I understand!—Poor Rose,
  From blame her weakness is not free!—
The best, perchance, among her beaux,
  Her father *made her* marry me.

We boast our daughters have a choice,
  Yet many a daughter is but sold,
And seems to give consenting voice,—
  The greatest cheat performed for gold!

I've met with marrying mammas,
  Their clever plotting have detected;
Match-making schemes among papas,
  This heartless work I ne'er suspected!

The want that struck me, this explains—
  She sees her future cold and blank;
Wives without love are slaves in chains,
  And husbands hear the fetters clank!

How could I wed a giddy wife
  Whose tastes must ever clash with mine!
And cast my happiness for life
  An offering at her beauty's shrine!

I cannot such disgrace endure
  As that she made me bear last night;
I scarcely even feel secure,
  With her behavior free and light!

We went to dine at Lady Græme's—
  My wife appears a finished flirt!
Her conduct greatly shocked Sir James,
  I felt provoked with her—and hurt!

At dinner, at Sir James's side,
She took her post as honored bride,
And filled it with a pretty grace,
A sweet bewilderment of face. —
But after, in the drawing room,
  Resolved was she to make display!
I know not how she could presume
  To act in that outrageous way,
And with loud merriment to be
To all around her gay and free!—
A knot of men beside her chair
  Assembled, first, to joke and laugh,
Which she approved, with lively air,
  And joined them in their fun and chaff!
I talked apart with Lady Græme,
But there the boisterous laughter came.
It made me feel ashamed and vexed!—
But scarce prepared for what was next!
For then, a tall and languid swell
  With easy carelessness advanced—

He seemed to know her passing well!—
  It was the man with whom she danced!
Upon her easy-chair he leant,
  And spoke to her in lowered tone
With cool effrontery—as bent
  To make her his acquaintance own.
She raised her eyes as if to speak,
With mantling blushes on her cheek.
I caught Sir James's wondering look,
And other people notice took.—
Then she became confused, and shy,
  Got up—to move away, I thought,—
Sat down again without reply,—
  And what it meant in vain I sought!—
I wonder what he could have said
To make her blush so deep a red!
But she recovered from her fright,
  And whispered answers back to him—
Perchance some nonsense, gay and light—
  He took advantage of her whim,

And there beside her down he sat
For a long, confidential chat,
And so engrossed and pleased are they,
'A pair of lovers' one would say!

It seems her great delight to be
  Agreeable to all around,
And none so bold, and none so free,
  But she can meet them on their ground!—
How dare she in this way behave,
Dishonoring the name I gave!
And drawing all regards upon her
As if she gloried in dishonor!
We said good night to Lady Græme
And then, together, home we came
Home! Is it any home to me,
  Or is there any hope in life,
When all my happiness I see
  Intrusted to a flirting wife?

I did not speak as back we drove,
  I could not trust myself to speak,
My anger for the mastery strove
  At thought of her immodest freak.-
Yet with my passions in a stir
I sought to make excuse for her.

She is but young, she does not know
  How quick the world will ill impute;
My duty it should be to show,
  And save her from this bitter fruit.
If she could love me more discreet
That love would make her.—Ah! to meet
This fond assurance in her eyes,
And find her henceforth good and wise!

I grieve that we are kept apart!—
I longed to take her to my heart!
My just vexation I repressed—
  No evil thought had she in mind,

Her childish giddiness transgressed—
  I struggled to be calm and kind.

I found her in her dressing-gown—
With all her golden hair let down,
And watched her while she brushed her hair,
And wished she was as good as fair !

I asked her if she ever thinks—
From serious questions Rosa shrinks,
And the more earnest I may be
The more ridiculous is she—
She 'thought she'd liked to give a ball,'
And 'not to be reproved at all.'

I was determined, and I spoke
  Of all the cares and hopes of life,
And would not let a silly joke
  Prevent my duty to my wife ;

But all across the grain it went,
For still on mocking was she bent,
And said, with saucy-glancing eyes,
She'd rather far be fair than wise!
And begged while young to be but gay,
And like a merry kitten play.—
Her mockery some time I stood
And tried to speak to her for good;
But she, with answers vain and light,
  And still disposed to play the fool,
My rallied patience put to flight,
  And I was neither kind nor cool!
I thought of all the galling shame
  That she so lately made me bear—
I thought of my long-honored name—
  And of the friends that saw her there,
And passed her conduct in review—
And as I thought my anger grew!
Then I declared she should not be
With any man or men so free;

Betraying all my holy trust,
  Forgetful of her marriage vow,
Trailing my honor in the dust,
  And bringing shame upon her brow!—
Why did she blush, that man to meet?
  I asked. How did she dare to flirt?—
With levity she strove to treat
  The matter, giving answer pert.
But I insisted on reply—
  Without reply I would not go,
And though she then began to cry,
  Where she had met that man I'd know!
I said she should not pass the door
  Till she had answered me, and told
Where she had met that man before!
  At length—when she had grown less bold—
She 'met him at Sir James's ball,'—
  Of course, she did!—'Where else, beside?'—
She did not know.—'Where else?' I cried.
And then, 'Ah! nowhere else at all.'—

She did not tell the truth, I know!
  I said, 'You've told a lie, I fear!'—
  I waited not excuse to hear!—
From bad to worse thus matters go—
My anger great!—And wider grows
The breach I vainly sought to close!

PART III.

AWAY ! away !—across the sea !
  Away, alone !—pursued by Care !
Away from home, if home it be !—
  Far, far away !—no matter where !

To find our idols made of clay !
  To find our fondest hopes deceived !—
She, whom I thought as clear as day !
  She, whom I trusted and believed !

How could I love so frail a thing !
  How could I see great promise there !—
The more the hope the sharper sting
  If hope gives place to blank despair !

One wretched day when I returned
  That Captain by her side I found!
My righteous anger fiercely burned!
  I could have struck him to the ground!

He had presumed to call on her,
  And she received him, though alone,—
I vainly hoped she would defer
  To me; although my wish was known.

Her hair was hanging all astray—
  She made excuse, she 'was asleep'—
I see her as I saw that day!—
  I scarcely could my temper keep!

I said, 'There must be some mistake'—
  I strove to seem polite and cool—
'Calls gentlemen did never make
  When I was out'—for such our rule.

Fitz-Maurice tried to talk, I know,
  I did not heed him, what he meant—
I'd have no words—I bade him go—
  I showed the door, and then he went.

He went!—and there my erring wife
  Confessed the many wrongs she'd done.—
That was the moment in my life
  That had not either hope or sun!

For, so her revelations ran,
  Not only had she let him call,
But had been flirting with this man
  Since she first met him at the ball.—

She said, she wandered out alone
  The day that followed on that dance,
Of indoor life so weary grown—
  And she had met him there by chance;

Had met him in a public walk
  Where she had unattended gone;
Had let him stay with her and talk—
  And so her dreadful tale went on.

She found her lonely hours were dull—
  Was glad when he had called before—
Some tempting pleasure sought to cull—
  And met him still, outside the door.

At home, alone, she could not stay,
  With nothing that she liked to do—
Not only did she disobey,
  But she had uttered falsehood too ;—

Had lied to me from fear, she said,
  Had tried before to tell the truth—
She did not like the days she led,
  She wanted pleasure in her youth ;

And must gad out, and flirt, and chat—
  Such was her happiness in life !—
My heart stopped beating !—Then, was that
  The woman I had made my wife !

Was that my beautiful ideal
  Whom I had worshipped, loved, believed !
And was there nothing true or real,—
  Was all my trusting love deceived !

My blood surged back !—In rage and pain
  Some hurried, angry words I spoke ;
Said, I could ne'er believe again,
  Or trust her—and away I broke.

With bitter thoughts I paced my room !
  I knew not how the hours went past,
Till in the midst of darkest gloom
  One brighter gleam broke in at last.

I would away !—When far from her
  I might again be strong and brave !—
At once I acted on the spur
  This sudden resolution gave.

Our house had ill accounts received
  From Spain, and some one needs must go—
I'd take the duty !—I believed
  It would divert me from my woe.

To office, therefore, down I went
  And said that I would go to Spain—
And all the day attention lent
  While this affair was put in train.

All the long day, through business hours,
  I recognized a two-fold mind,
The one exerting usual pow'rs
  The other holding back behind,

About that dreadful tale to lurk !—
  Like watch on rescued body found
Which, sympathetic, stopped its work
  And marks the time the man was drowned.

So it had stopped, stopped at the minute
  When she her revelation made,
And blankly viewed the horrors in it,
  Nor saw a chance of coming aid.—

I felt that I could cry aloud,
  Could shout till all the city heard;
That I could tell the startled crowd
  There was no faith in human word!

No trust in oath, in holiest bond,
  No surety anywhere on earth !—
That they must look this world beyond
  For truth and honor, faith and worth !—

And still the busy day sped on,
  And still I did my duty there,
And wished the weary hours were gone
  That I might give me to despair !—

My hope is lost, my life is wrecked !—
  I strike upon a hidden rock
Where nought of danger I suspect—
  Nor know it till I feel the shock !

But girls when trained to flirt, and catch
  The wealthiest man that takes the bait,
Will, after they have made the match,
  Flirt on for pastime, tempting fate.

And wives who love not ere they wed
  How like they are to go astray,
To be by each false light misled,
  To wander from the safer way.—

If she admires a dashing beau
  How could she wed a man like me ?—
If time for us once more might flow
  I'd keep from all this turmoil free !

A letter from Sir James, to say,
They take my wife with them to stay.
Now this is very good indeed;
This is a friend, a friend in need!—
It has removed an anxious care
To know that she is sheltered there!—
They do me a most friendly turn,
  For I so hurriedly took flight
  I left it all to him!—I'll write,
And thank him for his kind concern.

Three weary months ! Oh ! who shall tell
  The sickening weight of woe they bore !
The constant sense of loneliness,
  The want of all beheld no more,
The yearning of the secret soul
  That shrank from every scene of mirth,
The vacant eye, the heedless ear,
  The aching void, the bosom's dearth !

Three long, long months, and day by day
  A canker preying on the heart !
The gnawing tooth of memory,
  The form of her from whom I part.
Without—no thing but beauty there,
  Within—a sense of dreary cold
To bind each happier impulse down,
  And freeze the spirit by its hold !

Three trailing months! and through their course
  This changeless load of care and gloom,
This living death, this dying life—
  The festive board is like a tomb,
The brightest sunshine seems but chill,
  A murky mist the lightest air,
The bridal peal a passing knell,
  And hope itself is like despair!

I'm back again! I wrote to say
They might expect me back to-day,
And that I hoped my wife would be
Home in our house to welcome me.
Oh, how I longed to see her face!—
And how I dreaded, too, to trace
Some sign of reticence and care
To doom me still to dark despair—
To prove I had a rival there?

I never felt such qualms before!
I hardly dared to pass the door,
And when I saw her in the room
I was afraid to meet my doom!—
I knew not what to say or do,
  I did not venture to be fond—

Oh! is she faithful? Is she true?
  Or must I evermore despond?

Like simple friends, alas! we met—
She did not seem to feel regret,
Nor did she say that she was glad
To see me back—I wish she had!—
Some slight remark about the train,
And we were silent once again.—
She scarcely even looked at me,
And then she poured me out some tea,
And then we spoke of Lady Græme—
But still the talk reluctant came;
For she was frightened and constrained,
And I was sorely grieved and pained.

What have I done to frighten Rose?—
  She must have thought me most severe!—
She cannot love me!—All she shows
  Is sad restraint and childish fear.

I was half mad that wretched day!—
  I feel I acted much amiss
To rush so savagely away;—
  I know not how to tell her this!

It was but giddiness and youth
  Brought that about which made me go!—
I'm now convinced she spoke the truth,
  And let me all her trespass know.

In her sweet eyes there dwells a look
  Of almost angel innocence,
I read her soul as 'twere a book:
  I take some little comfort hence;—

The wretched man that drew her on,
  For him, at least, she did not care—
She only wanted to be gone
  With anybody, anywhere.

But yet her conduct was not nice,
  Nor nice the fruit from seed she's sown!—
Sir James came here to give advice,—
  He'd better leave the thing alone!

He undertook to lecture me!
  And told me to amuse my wife,
To let her run about and see
  The Town, and lead a merry life!

His grand array I strove to rout,
  But still he would the attack renew,
And so at last I turned him out—
  And then I felt more sorry, too!

For he and I were firmest friends,
  Now, also, I am in his debt.—
I know not how to make amends—
  I scarcely can forgive him yet!

How could he come and dare advise,
  And tell me what I ought to do!
My wife's behavior criticise,
  And preach about her beauty too!

How dare he tell me she is vain,—
  And my unkindness then infer,
And say her love I should retain
  If I would stoop to flatter her!—

I found my wife was seated there !—
  This makes the matter quite absurd !—
Rosa was resting in a chair
  And all this conversation heard !

But people have a right to prate,
  And we must be content to hear—
O ! how the whole affair I hate
  That makes them talk and interfere !

That made me rush away to Spain,
  And my poor wife afraid of me ;
And keeps us when I come again
  As distant as we well can be.

Her father forced from her—consent,
  But could not force her feelings too !—
And bitterly must I repent
  That he my hasty offer drew !

I felt convinced he sounded me:—
  But when our motives pure we know,
From dread too nice we might be free,
  And trust to time our truth to show.

His was a most unworthy part—
  To sacrifice his daughter's life,
To give her hand without a heart,
  And make her in but name a wife!

Yet if for much of love you plead,
  The world will talk about romance—
Position is the thing to heed;
  Affection—that may come by chance.

Love-matches—they are held in scorn!
  The best that offers you should take!
And some poor daughters seem but born
  To try a wealthy match to make!

Poor Rosa spoke to me to-night
And said she wishes to do right,
And she desires to please me too,
If I will tell her what to do.
I do believe she seeks the good—
I said I'd help her if I could—
But while my hopes were springing up,
She quickly dashed away the cup!
For having seriously begun,
Off at a tangent she must run,
And talk such nonsense with such glee,
I found she'd made a fool of me!
She had the shocking taste to say
  There is in doing wrong a charm—
She makes me wonder every day
  She has not come to greater harm!

She is so giddy and so vain,
From comment I could not refrain.—
She refuge in her beauty took,
And tried to conquer by a look;
This made me say in angry tone
I did not care for looks alone,
She might as well cast pearls to swine
As angle thus for love of mine;
For looks give promise, which she breaks—
And still by looks again re-makes.

How cruel was the wrong she did,
  Pretending love she could not feel;
Down in my soul the wound lies hid,
  Too deep, alas! for time to heal!

I danced with her to-night—a waltz—
  A foolish thing it was to do,
It made me feel how poor and false
  The life we lead; for as I flew
Around with Rosa in my arms,
  The creature whom I love so much,
Her happy smiles, her youthful charms,
  The gay delight of step and touch
Bewildered me, and made the measure
  A most enthralling, maddening pleasure!

Of course, it is not etiquette—
  One's own dear wife—I know 'twas wrong
To dance with Rose to-night—but yet
  Excuses which I make are strong.—

A ball there was at Mrs. Payne's
  And I had taken Rosa there,
For gladly would I make the chains
  Less heavy, which my wife must wear ;—
And as she loves to gad about
I feel I ought to take her out.

A waltz was forming, and the band
  Struck up a most inviting strain—
A doorway watching as I stand,
  I see her enter there again ;
And with her comes the empty fop
  With whom she vexed me much before,
And by his side she would not stop,
  She left him just within the door.
He sought to lead her to the dance,
  But she repulsed his vain advance.

She left him and she crossed to me,
  Upon my arm she placed her hand,

And I was pleased at this degree
  Of wifely trust—and half unmanned,—
And knowing how she loves the dance,
  I put my arm about her waist,
And mid the couples we advance.—
  I did it thoughtlessly, in haste ;
'Twas very foolish on my part,
It woke such longing in my heart !

The waltz itself it was not bad ;
  To dance with her was best of all,
She looked so happy and so glad,
  She thought it an enchanting ball !—
What ecstasy I felt to-night !
  To dance with Rosa is delightful !
Though some might wonder at the sight,
  And that poor man be vexed and spiteful
To see her pleased though she discards
Captain Fitz-Maurice, of the Guards.

Dear Rosa twitted me to-day
  With my performance at the ball;
And, in reply, what could I say?
  I scarce could answer her at all!—
She does not love, and cannot know
  Of inly-bleeding wounds, the woe!—
My disappointed life drags on;
  A breathing image at its side!
My early hope of joy is gone—
  A faultless statue for a bride!—
One look of love that beamed on me
  Would better than all beauty be!

One time I was informed by Rose—
  To some extent I own 'tis true—
That if to marry her I chose,
  I ought to make her happy too.—
We've nought in common in our lives,
  Our tastes and interests never blend!
I've ordered broughams for her drives,
  Unless she goes with some kind friend,
For I am many hours away
And she is lonely in the day.
She, in herself, has few resources,
  Nothing to occupy her mind.—
If girls went through severer courses
  Of study, would it leave behind
A something to fall back upon?
  A love of deep and earnest books,

Now that the old regime is gone
Which made them—housewives, doctors, cooks ?—
She has so little but her beauty !
I scarcely know what I can do—
I'm anxious to perform my duty—
I'd 'make her happy' if I knew !
But she is frightened ! I was hard
And harsh with her !—so said Sir James.
I've latterly been on my guard.
I fully recognise her claims.—
It was before I went to Spain ;
If those dark days came once again
I would be gentler ! She should see
Her faults and her I separate ;
But she has grown afraid of me—
My good intentions come too late !

Able to hold a pen once more !—
  But many months have passed away
Since I an entry made before,
  And now how much I have to say !
And all I say is glad and bright,
For all the wrong has turned to right !

I well remember that sad life
  When Rose and I were kept apart,
But now my loving little wife
  Is one with me in hand and heart !
I've won my wife !—I know not how !—
But nothing's sad or gloomy now !

There was a weary time of pain
  And heavily the days went by,

I seemed to doze and wake again,
And lay in bed I knew not why ;—
At times I did not know or care
What happened then, or who was there.

Until one evening I awoke
And saw dear Rosa near the bed.
I gazed upon the sun, and spoke,
Remarking it was very red.
And then she came and looked at me,
And something, when she looks, I see!

What was it in her glorious eyes
Had taken up its residence ?—
It filled me, first, with strange surprise,
And then, with happiness intense,
For while I looked I read aright—
'Twas love for me that gave their light !

Oh! happy days in my sick room
  When this glad news had been received!
It banished care, it banished gloom—
  In pain itself I scarce believed,
For I could think of nothing then
  But love—that came I know not when!

And oh! the rapture of the kiss
  She laid upon my thirsty lips!
It was the essence of all bliss,
  It tingled to my finger-tips!—
Its taste from hope it did not borrow,
For it was joy come out of sorrow!

And then she told me all the tale,
  That I had long been very ill—
And still her fears for me prevail,
  She says I must be careful still—
And when they brought me home, she said,
At first the doctors thought me dead.

And now she will not let me talk—
  She always liked to talk to me!—
And when I first essayed to walk,
  My efforts she was scared to see.—
She strives to be the sternest nurse
That ever made a patient worse!

I love the serious, sober way
  In which she would command assume,
I love her simple dress of grey
  Which does not rustle in the room.
But to be stern!—she cannot do it!
Her gentleness comes smiling through it!

They tell me—but all that I knew—
  When passing by, in neighboring street,
A child had fallen, and I flew
  To save him from the horses' feet.
This I remembered very well,
And one thing more *they* could not tell.

That when on level of my eyes
  Those horses' ugly hoofs I see
Immense ones are they, thrice the size
  Of any hoofs beheld by me!
Some reason for the fact I sought,
And this became my latest thought.

Then was a time not all a blank,
  For I was conscious of distress;
From movement and from noise I shrank,
  I suffered dreadful weariness,
But scarcely knew what passed around—
Or how I got from off the ground.

That dancing paper on the wall—
  I think that paper I'll remove—
I could not add it up at all,
  Or if I did it would not prove!
I hate a pattern which will go
Diagonally to and fro!

A clock there was that struck the hour,
  And seemed to strike them all the same,
And, somehow, had a sort of pow'r
  To make them strike a person's name.—
That name in one sweet cadence fell,
And it was always—Rosa Bell.

From all these troubles, vague and true,
  I woke to find dear Rosa mine!—
And were the thing again to do
  I'd do it, and would not repine!
Better the sickness o'er and o'er,
Than lead the life we led before!

I told my darling wife to-day
  Of all the trouble and the pain
In that dark time, now far away,
  When love could find no love again ;—
Of all those hard and bitter days,
When we were pulling different ways ;
And all my grief, long unassuaged,
And the internal war that raged
Taking my heart for battle-ground
And leaving harder than it found.—
She looked at me with loving eyes,
  But in those eyes were tears as well,
And more of sorrow than surprise ;
  I kissed the tears before they fell !—
What joy when undivided life
Is led by loving man and wife !

At work again, and well and strong,
And happy as the day is long !—
And rather long it seemed at first
  To be away from dearest Rose,
I'd been so petted and so nursed—
  But men must work—for so it goes,
And even with my charming wife
I should not like an idle life.

Some pleasant drives were those we had—
  And Rose admired my appetite !
One's convalescence is not bad
  With all around you gay and bright.

This joyful thing, too, happened there—
  Sir James came up to speak to me

When I was propped in easy chair;—
  He said he was quite glad to see
That I was getting round at last—
And thus our little feud blew past;
He shook me warmly by the hand—
  We both regretted friendship broken,
And each could other understand
  As if a thousand words were spoken.

The Medico, with solemn look,
Said, he must give me to the cook.
Why will some stupid men refuse
With cheerful air to tell good news?
One would have thought the undertaker
Was hinted at, and not the baker!

Dear Rosa read aloud to me—
  The City article, and stocks
She would attempt, but I could see
  She knows far more of gowns and frocks.

But sometimes, though, she'd rather chat,
And I did not object to that,
And learned to understand her ways
Much better than in former days.

My wife has taken to her books,
  And works with energy and zeal;
I must not have her spoil her looks,
  Nor let her work her roses steal.
Her studies may be very well,
But on her health they must not tell.

I took her home some pretty birds
  And much attached to them she grew;
She talks to them in broken words
  And they chirp back as if they knew!
I find she's very fond of pets—
Great pleasure from the things she gets.

She told me she had felt it hard
  To leave the country, and the air,
We've made a garden in the yard—
  I doubt if it will flourish there ;
She's proud enough, though, of her flow'rs—
And then she has such lonely hours !

What made her love me ? Who can tell !—
  It is a source of wonder still !
She could not love when I was well
  And grew to love when I was ill.
What could it be ?—I cannot think !
And yet from asking her I shrink.

What made her love me ?—Can it be
  Her love was by my love begot ?
Could it be anything in me ?
  Or good in her ? What was it ! What !—
Whate'er it was, I'm happy so,
And need not greatly care to know !

The birds and flowers are in danger !—
By an expected little stranger
Who some fine morning comes to town
They'll find themselves at once put down !—

Of Rose I take the greatest care,
She must have exercise and air ;
Dear Lady Græme is very nice
And gives her matronly advice.—
I think I'll hide her books away
And bring them out some other day—
Yes, I must see to that indeed,
I cannot let dear Rosa read,—
But yet we must not rashly thwart her.—
And will it be a son, or daughter ?

When Rosa took to loving me
  I'm sure we then were both agreed
No greater happiness could be
  And that of nought beside we'd need.
But now we very plainly see
  We then were only half content
And what we wanted, we agree,
  Was but the baby that is sent.

To Rose she is a new-found toy,
  And Rose is once again a child !—
She would have rather had a boy
  She said,—but then the baby smiled,
Or if she did not smile we took
For smiling that most funny look—

And I am sure Rose would not change her
For any other little stranger!

She is to me a droll set out!
I scarcely know what I'm about
When her fond mother makes me 'take her,'—
  I'd almost rather 'take' a pill,
For fear to pieces I should shake her,
  Or do her some tremendous ill!

What great responsibilities
  Attach to this my new condition!
I look with due civilities
On 'Woman's Rights,' and 'Woman's Mission;'

And 'Women's Property;' and laws
  For giving them consideration;—
There surely ought to be a clause
  That they should govern all the nation!

For women always govern men;
  And then, beside,—we have a queen;
And—lady-doctors, too; and then,—
  We know that women's wits are keen.

And now they're all to be so skilled,
  Boys will be beaten by a head!—
But, in whatever they are drilled,
  Pray teach them this before they wed:—

That *loveless marriage is a crime,*
  That *flirting is a 'false pretence.'*—
This is the evil of the time;
  And rank the crops that spring up hence.

Now that I own a little daughter,
  How can I tell what lies in store?
How many lovers she may slaughter—
  And then turn round and ask for more!

No! she shall be sincere and true,
  And like her mother as she grows,
But better trained, and taught to do
  Not quite the same as did dear Rose.

For though at last it turned out well,
  And she her husband learnt to love,
It was a chance !—No Major Bell
  Shall train this pretty nestling dove.

The system surely has been shaped
  To lead to misery and sin !
I feel I narrowly escaped
  A quagmire sucking many in.

That time of agony in Spain ?—
  Though smooth at last the troubled water
Those stormy days must still remain,—
  Her work not such, my little daughter !

No ; though I may be much derided,
  I'll have my way with this, my own,
And on one point I am decided—
  My babe shall wed for love alone !

Nor shall this second Rosa be
  A flirt, whatever else they make her!
Rather than have her that, I'd see—
  The baby-farmer come and take her!

We will not care for gain and greed,
  Though sought by greatest in the land!—
But, as her inclinations lead
  So goes my little daughter's hand!

We have authority for this—
  And let us copy from above;—
And may that marriage end in bliss,
  The fruit alone of mutual love!

www.ingramcontent.com/pod-product-compliance
Lightning Source LLC
LaVergne TN
LVHW021413110826
845150LV00007B/1905